PUT YOUR PEN
— TO —
PAPER

20 BOOK WRITING STRATEGIES THAT WORK

Kennisha Griffin

Founder/CEO of Create and Blossom Literary Studios

PUT YOUR PEN TO PAPER

Published by Create and Blossom Literary Studios

Copyright 2023 © Create and Blossom Studios

ISBN hardcover: 978-1-945304-92-7

ISBN paperback: 978-1-945403-89-7

All material is the original work of Kennisha Griffin and is not authorized to be copied without the author's permission.

Create and Blossom Literary Studios

901 S. Hewitt Dr.

P.O. Box 63

Hewitt, Texas 76643

www.createandblossomstudios.com

admin@createandblossomstudios.com

Cover Photography by Kennisha Griffin

Produced by Create and Blossom Literary Studios

Cover Art and Interior Design by Xee Designs

Printed in the United States of America

TABLE OF CONTENTS

Reviews v

Thank You vii

Introduction xi

CHAPTER ONE: ENCOURAGEMENT TO BECOME AN AUTHOR: JUST SAY YES! 1

CHAPTER TWO: LET'S BEGIN WRITING 7

CHAPTER THREE: PLANNING YOUR WRITING STRATEGY 11

CHAPTER FOUR: THE IMPORTANCE OF SHIFTING YOUR MINDSET 17

CHAPTER FIVE: UNLEASH YOUR UNIQUE WRITING STYLE: TIPS TO DISCOVER YOUR VOICE 23

CHAPTER SIX: STAYING MOTIVATED 27

CHAPTER SEVEN: BE YOUR OWN BIGGEST SUPPORTER 33

CHAPTER EIGHT: SHARPEN YOUR WRITING SKILLS TO COMPLETE YOUR BOOK 37

CHAPTER NINE: THE IMPORTANCE OF GENUINE CONNECTIONS 43

CHAPTER TEN: OVERCOMING WRITER'S BLOCK 49

CHAPTER ELEVEN: ACHIEVING YOUR GOAL OF COMPLETING YOUR BOOK: PROPER TIME MANAGEMENT IS KEY 55

CHAPTER TWELVE: OVERCOMING WRITING DISTRACTIONS 61

CHAPTER THIRTEEN: CREATING A WRITING PLAN 65

CHAPTER FOURTEEN: REMAINING TEACHABLE IS KEY TO COMPLETING YOUR BOOK 69

CHAPTER FIFTEEN: DISCOVERING YOUR AUDIENCE: TIPS AND TRICKS 73

CHAPTER SIXTEEN: ACHIEVING DISCIPLINE: TIPS FOR FINISHING WHAT YOU START 77

CHAPTER SEVENTEEN: SAVOR EACH CHAPTER, DON'T RUSH 81

CHAPTER EIGHTEEN: TIPS TO PREVENT OVERWHELM WHILE WRITING 85

CHAPTER NINETEEN: EMBRACING YOUR WRITING CALLING 91

CHAPTER TWENTY: A GUIDE TO MAKING MONEY AS A WRITER 95

BONUS CHAPTER: WHAT APPS TO USE TO WRITE YOUR BOOK 99

Thank you 103

Connect With Kennisha Griffin 104

REVIEWS

My sister, my friend Kennisha, has shared her love, spirit, passion, and wisdom with a room full of foster teens and managed to keep their attention as she spoke from the heart. I cannot wait to get her to come and share her love and experiences again. I'm so proud to call her a friend and a sister—blessings, as you bless all that know you.

-*Terrie Eley, YMCA Youth Development Director*

It's been an absolute pleasure working with Kennisha Create and Blossom Studios over the past few months of 2022 going into 2023 to help bring my autobiography to life. I could not have asked for a more consistent, genuine, and profound book coach to take the lead on my project. Her experience and knowledge of the industry are unmatched; without a doubt, I highly recommend Create and Blossom Studios.

-*Markus Cuttino, U.S. Army Veteran, Author*

www.cuttinosclubhouse.com

Kennisha has an extraordinary talent for the written word and is an expert in coaching others into putting their pen to paper, drawing out, defining, and developing others' raw thoughts and ideas into a book they will love and cherish. Kennisha is an actual author of her craft.

-*Piper Harris, Therapist, Owner, Untangled Mind, LLC, Author*

www.untangeledmind.net

Kennisha is a fantastic writer, author, and writing coach. I worked with her while writing my memoir, and she was instrumental in helping me get my words on paper and ultimately publish my memoir. As a coach, Kennisha is patient and skilled, and she has a knack for helping you pin down precisely what you're trying to say. I encourage you to use Kennisha for your next project!

-*Tiffany Dionne Kelly, Sex Trafficking Survivor, Author*

www.tiffanydionne.com

Kennisha helped me publish my first book and was a joy to work with! She helped navigate me through every step of the process in such a way as to ensure that I understood it all. I've also read one of her books, and she is as great an author as she is an editor/publisher! I highly recommend her!!

-*Georgette Jackson, Owner of Divine Rest, Inc, Author*

www.divinerestinc.org

Kennisha has been incredibly attentive and encouraging throughout my whole process and journey! I'm so thankful to have found her to walk alongside me. I can expect both kindness and honesty! Highly recommend!

-*Brittney Wardlaw, Owner, The Relationship Clinic, Author*

www.therelationshipclinic.com

THANK YOU

To every person who has trusted me with their extraordinary stories and allowed me to be a hint of encouragement in your life, thank you. Serving you has been an honor.

PUT YOUR PEN TO PAPER

INTRODUCTION

In 2020, amidst the chaos of the coronavirus pandemic, I launched "Create and Blossom Literary Studios" and my book "Put Your Pen to Paper." I created this resource to help aspiring writers find their voice and creativity during the lockdown. I even obtained an interview on FOX 44 KWKT and helped some writers publish their books. Being a multitasking mom of six children, four in school, made it a wild ride, but I achieved my goals while reentering the book writing and publishing space after a five-year break.

My book was designed to inspire and challenge writers to start and finish their books. The pandemic brought job loss and a sense of uncertainty, and I wanted to provide writers with the tools they could use to create a book that could also be financially lucrative. As a result, I released the first edition of my book. Unfortunately, the pandemic was too much to handle, and I had another baby, which forced me to put my company on hold.

After a busy season with my family, I realized I wanted to help authors again. On December 30th, 2022, I resigned from my position in higher education, which coincided with my daughter Karina's birthday. I began my new venture with Create and Blossom, working full-time. My first day on the job included a TV interview with Ally Kadlubar at KWTX, the CBS affiliate in Waco, TX. The first quarter of 2023 was filled with pleasant surprises, and every step of the way, I discovered new insights into writing and publishing that I can now share with others.

Reflecting on what made me successful when publishing books in Dallas, I realized I could connect with authors personally, using my knowledge and experience to help them craft stories that resonate with readers. I love the technical aspects of writing, and I enjoy offering advice and recommendations to aspiring authors. I love *storytelling*.

To me, personal stories are the most powerful. They shape, guide, and inspire us to learn, grow, and change. And so, in this revised edition, I wanted to be more transparent and share my writing journey. If you're writing a book and struggle with anxiety or fear of the unknown, know that you are not alone. I've experienced– and still sometimes experience– both anxiety and apprehension. But I'd love to communicate in this book that we can *still* move forward even with the challenges we face.

With this new edition, I aim to provide a resource aspiring writers could use to overcome their fears and concerns and accomplish their goals. As you read, take notes, and allow my words to help you discover your divine calling. It's time to put your pen to paper and share your story with the world.

CHAPTER ONE

ENCOURAGEMENT TO BECOME AN AUTHOR: JUST SAY YES!

When I started writing my debut novel, *Awakened*, I was overwhelmed with feelings of inadequacy. While I was sure that becoming an author was my calling, the fear of failing tried to hold me back. I've had a history of starting hobbies, such as ballet, piano, track, and ballroom dancing, without fully committing to them. I entered college during my junior year of high school, only danced ballet twice, and didn't try out for track due to a medical condition. I had developed a habit of starting things and never finishing them. I knew that if I wanted to succeed as an author, I would need to confront this pattern and conquer it. Overcoming any roadblocks and mastering writing techniques became my top priority. I was determined to do whatever it took to achieve my goal. Like a detective on a case, I started my journey by sleuthing for the perfect writing mentor.

When I first searched for a "writing mentor," I wasn't sure what to expect. I was looking for someone who had the experience, knowledge, and most importantly, *passion* for book writing. Feeling alone and uncertain, I was determined to find someone to guide me through the process. I was afraid of making mistakes on my own. After stumbling upon Tricia Goyer's blog, "My Writing Mentor," I knew I had found the right person. Tricia is a bestselling author with nearly 100 published books to her name. I signed up for her newsletter, sent her an email, and we've been friends ever since.

Thanks to Tricia, my writing has improved significantly. However, our work together also taught me about the challenges of traditional publishing – it's a highly competitive industry. Publishers are interested in authors with a strong platform to ensure book sales. Being an excellent writer is not always enough to guarantee success.

It was discouraging to learn that getting published can be arduous as I know how challenging rejection can be. It's already tough to manage feelings of inadequacy, and the prospect of waiting a decade for a publisher to take interest only exacerbates the pressure. But, the question remains: is it worth the wait? It's a difficult question; however, I firmly believe that with proper guidance and support, anyone can realize their writing aspirations. That's why I felt compelled to provide a solution for those who may want to independently publish their books.

Tricia may not realize it, but her journey has been a source of inspiration for me. Throughout her experience, she has demonstrated admirable resilience, tenacity, and courage. She never discouraged writers; instead, she motivated them to refine their skills and trust the calling that God has placed on their lives. Her outlook was ministry-focused, and she believed that traditional publication was not always the end goal. There are many opportunities in the publishing industry.

After much thought and prayer, I realized that there are many people out there with amazing stories to tell, but no platform to share them. They may not have thousands of followers on social media, nor anyone else in their lives who would be interested in their book. However, they are eager to share their experiences with the world for a greater purpose. That's why I decided to take action. As a creative storyteller, I want to help others share their stories too.

I believe that everyone's story is unique and valuable, regardless of their background or circumstances. By giving a voice to those who may not have one, I hope to create a more inclusive and diverse literary world. It's important to me that everyone has the opportunity to share their truth and be heard.

Through my work, I've had the privilege of helping many people bring their stories to life. It's a humbling experience to be trusted with someone's personal narrative, and I take that responsibility very seriously. I work closely with my clients to understand their vision and voice, and to ensure that their message is conveyed authentically.

I believe that storytelling has the power to connect us all, and that by sharing our stories, we can build empathy and understanding. So if you have a story to tell, but don't know where to start, know that you're not alone. There are people out there who want to help you share your story, and I'm one of them.

If you're feeling inadequate

Becoming an author can be an incredibly gratifying and satisfying career choice, but it is not without its obstacles.

One of the greatest challenges that authors frequently encounter is a sense of inadequacy. This sentiment can originate from various sources, such as self-doubt, critiques from others, and the pressure to consistently produce exceptional work.

Self-doubt is perhaps the most common cause of feeling inadequate as an author. It's easy to compare ourselves to other successful authors and feel like we're not measuring up. It's also easy to worry about rejection from publishers. However, it's important to remember that every author's journey is unique, and success can look different for everyone. Instead of comparing ourselves to others, we should focus on our own growth and progress as writers.

Criticism from others can also be a major source of feeling inadequate. It's not uncommon for authors to receive negative feedback or harsh reviews, and it can be difficult to not take it personally. However, it's important to remember that constructive criticism can be a valuable tool for improving our writing. Instead of dwelling on negative comments, try to use them as a learning opportunity and make adjustments to your writing as needed.

Finally, the pressure to produce great work can also contribute to feeling inadequate as an author. It's easy to feel like you're not living up to your potential or that your writing isn't as good as it should be. However, it's important to remember that writing is a process, and it takes time and effort to produce great work. Rather than focusing on the end result, try to enjoy the process of writing and trust that your hard work will pay off in the end.

Feeling inadequate as an author is a common experience, but it doesn't have to hold you back from achieving your goals. By focusing on your own growth, learning from criticism, and enjoying the writing process, you can overcome these feelings and become a successful author. Remember, every writer has their own journey, and it's up to you to make the most of yours.

What happens when you say yes

Saying yes is the first step, but it's more than simply acknowledging a goal. Saying yes requires critically examining all that's required and committing to completing the task before you type the first word. Saying yes is visualizing your book in your hands and not stopping until that vision becomes a reality. Saying yes is not letting anything get in your way.

Have you ever thought about writing a book? Perhaps you have a story to tell, expertise to share, or a passion project that you've been working on. Whatever the reason may be, saying yes to writing your book can be a life-changing decision.

Writing a book can be a daunting task, especially if you've never done it before. However, the benefits of writing a book far outweigh the challenges. For starters, writing a book allows you to share your unique perspective with the world. It gives you the opportunity to connect with readers on a deep and meaningful level, and potentially inspire them to take action or make positive changes in their lives.

In addition to the personal satisfaction of writing a book, there are also tangible benefits to consider. A well-written book can open doors to new opportunities, such as speaking engagements, media interviews, and consulting gigs. It can also establish you as an authority in your field and help you build a personal brand.

Of course, writing a book is easier said than done. It takes time, effort, and dedication to bring your vision to life.

However, the key is to start small and take it one step at a time. Set aside time each day to write, even if it's just a few hundred words. Celebrate your milestones along the way, such as finishing a chapter or reaching a certain word count. And most importantly, don't give up. Remember why you said yes to writing your book in the first place, and let that be your motivation to keep going.

In conclusion, saying yes to writing your book can be a transformative experience. It allows you to share your story, connect with readers, and potentially open doors to new opportunities. While the journey may be challenging at times, the rewards are well worth it. All you have to do is say yes.

CHAPTER TWO

LET'S BEGIN WRITING

Before we start working together, my coaching clients and I have an initial discussion about their goals. Understanding their vision is essential to me, as it provides me with a clear understanding of what they want. This insight allows me to determine their requirements and what they need before they start assembling or writing their books.

Some clients come with pre-written content from their journals, diaries, blog posts, or social media. Although sharing your hard work with a stranger can be difficult, it is a crucial step in our process. In my experience, content is content, regardless of where it came from. Having something to work with is better than having nothing.

But don't worry if you don't have any prior materials. It's possible to have excellent book ideas without anything written down on paper. In this chapter, I'll discuss how to start writing your book, with or without existing content.

Like many aspiring writers, I had previously published content on my blog, "The Ready Writer." I had accumulated around 10 to 12 posts and decided to use them as the foundation for my initial book. It seemed like a logical step to take. I had existing legally owned content that I could expand upon by adding more details, a few stories, and scripture references that were relevant to each chapter. And voila! My manuscript was complete.

Looking back at my first book, written as a young 20-something-year-old with minimal writing experience, I cringe at some of my earlier work. Despite this, I'm proud of my determination and appreciate the journey. Blogging played a significant role in enhancing my writing skills. As the old saying goes, "Don't be a writer- be writing." That's precisely what I did, and I embraced the community that came with blogging.

If you have content

Writing a book can be challenging, but using your own blogs and social media content can make the process easier. By repurposing your existing content, you can save time and effort while still creating a high-quality book.

1. **Choose a theme:** Look through your blog and social media posts and choose a common theme that you've written about. This could be anything from travel to cooking to personal growth. By selecting a theme, you can ensure that your book has a cohesive message and structure. For my first book, my central theme was faith and resilience.

2. **Organize your content:** Once you've chosen your theme, organize all of your relevant blog posts and social media updates into a cohesive outline. This

will help you to see where there are gaps in your content and where you need to do more writing.

3. **Fill in the gaps:** Now that you have your outline, fill in any gaps in your content by writing new blog posts or social media updates. This will ensure that your book is comprehensive and covers all aspects of your chosen theme.

By repurposing your existing blog and social media content, you can write a book that is both high-quality and efficient to create. With a little organization and editing, you can turn your writing into a book that you can be proud of.

If you don't have content

When writers first ask me where they should start writing I normally tell them wherever they would like. Now I know that might sound strange, but the truth is there is no perfect place to begin in a book especially if it is your first draft and if it is a non-fiction book. Please also note that if you are writing a novel, your chapter one can easily become chapter five. Your manuscript may go through several layers of edits. You may go back and change and want to add something different at the beginning of your book and that's okay! So, inhale a sigh of relief and don't apply any pressure. The truth is, you can begin by simply picking up your pen. Here's how:

First, start by brainstorming your ideas. What is the main message you want to convey in this chapter? What are the key points you want to make? Write down everything that comes to mind, even if it seems trivial or disconnected at first. This will help you to organize your thoughts and begin to see patterns and connections.

Next, create an outline. This doesn't have to be a formal, structured outline, but rather a rough sketch of the main sections of your chapter and the key points you want to make within each section. This will help you to stay focused and on track as you write, and will also make it easier to revise and edit later on.

Once you have your ideas and outline in place, it's time to start writing. Don't worry about making everything perfect on the first try - just focus on getting your thoughts down on paper. You can always go back and revise later. And remember, it's okay to start with the middle or end of the chapter, and then work on the beginning after you have a better sense of the overall flow and structure.

CHAPTER THREE

PLANNING YOUR WRITING STRATEGY

It wasn't until I began working with my first clients that I realized the significance of having a writing plan. I discovered that many of them were facing a common challenge. Some had plenty of content they could use, such as old journals filled with private thoughts and visions. They sought my help in organizing their material. Others, however, struggled to find their creative direction. They weren't sure how to begin, what to talk about, or how to structure their thoughts. As a result, I decided to create a writing plan for my clients as a way to help them overcome their obstacles.

The writing plan became an entire program module that my clients could follow throughout our writing process. I included what we focused on during each coaching session, their writing goals, and the tasks they needed to complete. One of my clients, a young lady working on a memoir, had difficulties organizing her book. She had so many pieces of content that didn't seem to fit together. After reviewing each chapter, I realized that she needed to rethink the structure of her book. That's when I decided to include a writing plan to help connect the dots for my clients.

Creating a Writing Plan: Key Components

If you're struggling with writing, a writing plan can be incredibly helpful. It's a document that outlines the necessary steps to complete your writing project. Here are some key components to consider when creating your writing plan:

Define your project:

Identify what type of writing you want to create, such as a novel, memoir, or research paper.

Once you have identified the type of writing you want to create, it's important to define the scope of your project. This means deciding on the length of your work, the tone and style you want to use, and the audience you are writing for. You should also consider your goals for the project and how you plan to achieve them. This might involve conducting research, creating an outline or plan, or seeking feedback from others. Remember, writing is a process, and it takes time and effort to create a polished and effective piece of work. So, take the time to define your project and set yourself up for success.

Establish your goals:

Determine the goals for your writing project, such as the word count, the number of chapters, or the deadline for completion.

Once you have established your goals, it's important to create a plan to achieve them. This may include breaking down your project into smaller, more manageable tasks, creating a timeline or schedule, and setting milestones to track your progress. It's also helpful to establish a routine or schedule for your writing, as this can help you stay focused and motivated. Additionally, it's important to consider your audience and the purpose of your writing, as this can help you tailor your message and ensure that it is effective and engaging. Finally, don't forget to seek feedback and support from others, as this can help you refine your writing and stay on track towards achieving your goals.

Develop a timeline:

Create a timeline that outlines when you will complete each section of your writing project.

Creating a timeline is a great way to stay organized and on track with your writing project. First, start by breaking down your project into smaller sections, such as researching, outlining, writing, and editing. Then, assign a realistic deadline for each section based on your schedule and the overall timeline for the project.

For example, you may want to spend a week on researching, two weeks on outlining, four weeks on writing, and one week on editing. Once you have your deadlines set, create a visual timeline, such as a calendar or a spreadsheet, to keep track of your progress and ensure that you stay on schedule. Remember to be flexible and adjust your timeline as needed, but try to stick to your deadlines as much as possible. With a clear timeline in place, you'll be able to tackle your writing project with confidence and ease.

Determine your writing process:

Decide if you will write in chunks or all at once, and whether you will write in chronological order or jump around.

When it comes to writing, there is no one-size-fits-all approach. Each writer has their own unique style and preferences. One of the biggest decisions you will need to make as a writer is how you will tackle your writing project. One factor to consider is whether you will write in chunks or all at once.

Writing in chunks involves breaking your writing project into smaller, more manageable pieces. This can be helpful if you have a busy schedule or struggle with writer's block. You can set aside time to work on a specific chunk of your project, rather than feeling overwhelmed by the entire project at once.

On the other hand, some writers prefer to write all at once. This approach may work well if you are someone who likes to get into a flow state and thrive on momentum. If you have a clear idea of where your writing project is going and enjoy working for longer stretches of time, this approach may be right for you.

Another decision to make is whether you will write in chronological order or jump around. Writing in chronological order means starting at the beginning of your project and working your way through to the end. This can be helpful if you have a clear idea of the structure of your project and want to follow a logical sequence.

However, some writers find it more helpful to jump around. This approach involves working on different parts of your project at different times, rather than trying to write everything in order. This can be helpful if you are struggling with a particular section or need a change of pace.

Ultimately, the best approach to writing will depend on your personal preferences, your writing style, and the specific demands of your project. Experiment with different methods until you find what works best for you.

By following these steps, you can create a writing plan that will help you stay focused and on track.

CHAPTER FOUR

THE IMPORTANCE OF SHIFTING YOUR MINDSET

I fully believe that pairing goals, desires and ambitions with the right mindset is critical for success. I also believe it's important to understand why you think the way that you do. Identify the fears and concerns, address them, and find solutions to overcome them. Some people may wonder why I spend so much time discussing the psychology of book writing. In this context, psychology is defined as the study of the mental characteristics and attitude of writers. The reason I focus here is because I believe there is a certain type of mindset that's required in order for writers to write a book. You need grit, determination, commitment, and an intense amount of focus. In my experience working with hundreds of authors, if any of these are lacking, there's a high probability that your book will not get completed. Some of the coolest experiences I've had are from authors who were determined to finish writing their books, no matter how much work needed to be done. Their mission was always their focal point, and they didn't let anyone get in the way of their goals.

One of my writing clients was a very old man who attended one of my workshops in Lewisville, Texas. As I stood in the front of the class scrolling through notes on my Ipad, I noticed him slowly walk in with a cane- the kind that had two handles on it. He inched his way at a turtles pace, while looking like a student who was overly prepared for class. His khaki pants were up past his belly button, held up with a tight belt that gripped his white polo shirt. His black thick eyeglass frames perfectly matched. He placed a folder full of paper on the table, sat back and took in a deep breath. It must have taken a lot for him to make it. I wondered if he was alone, if anyone accompanied him. He smiled. He sat. He waited.

I presented my presentation and the entire time he quietly sat there. No engagement. No participation. He tightly gripped his folder and paid attention to my lecture. After I was finished, I answered several questions, greeted several guests, and the room became empty- except he was still seated. I walked up to him, extended my hand, and asked, "What do you have there?" He explained how valuable each sheet of paper was- how he had been collecting pieces of his story to write them into a book one day. That day was the start of an amazing journey. After several meetings in the library, we walked through the entire process. His dream came true.

For over a decade, I've worked with many authors with different aspirations. Many write to use their stories to impact the world, share their wealth of knowledge, and make money. Many have established brands and wanted their books to make them an authority in their respective industries. And although they needed guidance to write their books, many had already asked themselves the right questions that created a fire in them that couldn't be extinguished. I love to witness their drive and determination., but it starts with asking and answering the right questions.

I learned the answer to these important questions in many of my first encounters with authors. Usually, in the beginning we discuss the book they want to write, their commitment to writing and completing it, the time they are willing to invest, and their overall purpose. Why do you want to write your book? I love to hear this answer because it varies for so many people. In this chapter, we'll discuss the three important questions I believe every aspiring author should ask themselves.

Why do you want to write this book?

When you sit down to write a book, it's important to have a clear understanding of its purpose. This will guide you in making decisions about everything from the tone and style of your writing to the topics you cover. The purpose of your book can be multifaceted, and may include educating your readers, sharing your personal experiences, or entertaining them with a compelling story.

One important aspect of understanding the purpose of your book is identifying your target audience. Who do you want to read your book, and why? Is your book aimed at a specific demographic, such as young adults or seniors? Are you hoping to reach people with particular interests or backgrounds? By understanding your target audience, you can tailor your writing to their needs and preferences, and ensure that your book resonates with them.

It's also worth considering the broader cultural and social context in which your book will be read. What is the current cultural climate, and how might your book fit into it? Are there particular messages or themes that are particularly relevant to your readers at this moment in time? Understanding the larger context in which your book will be received can help you to craft a narrative that feels timely and important, and that speaks directly to the concerns and interests of your readers.

You must know *your* why. This will help you answer other essential questions you'll need to answer– questions that will give you clarity and the courage and strength you'll need to finish writing your book.

Are you fully committed to completing your book?

Making the commitment to write a book can be a daunting task, but it is also an incredibly rewarding experience. Writing a book requires dedication, hard work, and perseverance. It is important to set realistic goals and establish a writing routine to ensure progress is being made. The first step in making this commitment is to decide on the type of book you want to write and the message you want to convey.

Once you have a clear idea of what you want to write, it is important to develop a writing plan. This includes setting aside dedicated time each day or week to write, and creating a space that is conducive to writing. It is also helpful to establish a routine that works for you, whether it's writing first thing in the morning or late at night. Remember, the key to success is consistency.

Finally, it is important to stay motivated throughout the writing process. This can be achieved by setting achievable goals, celebrating small successes along the way, and seeking support from other writers or writing groups. Remember, writing a book is a journey, and the commitment you make at the beginning will pay dividends in the end. So, take the first step today and make the commitment to write that book you've been dreaming of!

Will you create the time and space to write?

Creating the time and place to write a book is an essential part of the process of writing. Writing a book is a time-consuming and challenging task that requires full concentration and dedication. It is crucial to set aside a specific time and place to write to avoid distractions and maintain a consistent writing schedule. Having a designated place to write, whether it is a quiet corner in your home, a coffee shop, or a library, helps to create a writing routine and a sense of discipline.

Furthermore, creating a writing schedule and sticking to it helps to overcome writer's block and boosts productivity. Writing a book is not an easy task, and it can be easy to procrastinate or get distracted. However, by creating a writing schedule, it becomes easier to set goals and track progress. It also provides a sense of accountability, making it easier to stay on track and motivated. Overall, creating a time and place to write is an essential aspect of writing a book that can make the difference between success and failure.

CHAPTER FIVE

UNLEASH YOUR UNIQUE WRITING STYLE: TIPS TO DISCOVER YOUR VOICE

Have you ever read a book and immediately fell in love with the voice, as if you could hear the narrator sharing every single word to you over a cup of coffee at your favorite barista? Even if you've never heard the author's audio book recording, there are small nuances in their words that make you keenly aware that this is their book. Another author can't duplicate their tone and texture. This, ladies and gentleman, is their unique writing voice.

I first discovered my writing voice through blogging. This is one reason I believe in the power of blogging. I love the consistency and accountability it provides, however, I also love how writers get to know their writing voice and preferences through blogging. When I blogged, I learned more about my preferred writing style, and I felt comfortable with my writing quirks. I also resonated with others and that encouraged me. I could communicate in my own way and it was accepted. Have you ever considered your unique writing quirks?

Blogging also connected me with other writers and allowed me to observe their writing styles. It gave me the opportunity to ask myself questions like, "How would I say that?"

Finding your writing voice can be a challenging and ongoing process, but there are a few steps you can take to help discover and hone your unique style. First, it's important to read widely and often to expose yourself to different writing styles and techniques. This can include reading books, articles, and essays across genres and time periods.

Read different writing styles.

Reading different writing styles is important for aspiring authors because it exposes them to a variety of techniques, structures, and perspectives. By reading diverse works, writers can expand their understanding of storytelling, develop new ideas, and improve their own writing skills. It is important for writers to be well-read in order to create original and compelling works that stand out in a crowded market. You may ask "How so?" Keep in mind, when you're reading other books, you're learning from many titles that have gone through strict writing processes. That's right- class it in session. You're actually absorbing good skills from authors who put in a lot of time to create. They also worked with an established team to complete their book.

Write from personal experience and emotions.

Writing from personal experience and emotions can be a powerful tool for writers to convey their message in a way that resonates with their readers. By tapping into their own experiences, writers can create a sense of authenticity and relatability that can be hard to achieve through other means. When readers feel like the writer has lived through similar experiences or has felt the same emotions they have, it creates a connection that can be incredibly powerful and long-lasting. In addition, writing from personal experience and emotions help you tap into your authentic voice and make your writing more relatable and engaging. If you've ever wondered whether your unique writing voice is distracting or unlikable, you're not alone. This is a common concern for many aspiring authors.

In addition to creating a connection, writing from personal experience and emotions can also help writers discover new insights and perspectives. When writers delve into their own emotions and experiences, they often uncover new truths about themselves and the world around them. This can lead to a deeper understanding of the human experience and can inspire readers to do the same. By sharing their own stories and emotions, writers can encourage others to explore their own experiences and emotions, leading to a more empathetic and compassionate world.

Embrace feedback.

As a writer, it can be tempting to get defensive when receiving feedback on your work. However, embracing feedback is crucial to improving your writing skills. Feedback allows you to see your work from a different perspective and gain insight into how others interpret your writing. By listening to feedback, you can identify areas of weakness in your writing and learn how to improve them. This can ultimately help you become a better writer and produce higher quality work.

Additionally, feedback can help you connect with your audience. By understanding how your writing is perceived by others, you can make adjustments to better communicate your ideas and connect with your readers. This can lead to more engagement and a stronger connection with your audience, which is crucial for any writer. Overall, embracing feedback is an important step in improving your writing skills and connecting with your audience. Listening to constructive criticism can help you identify areas for improvement and refine your writing style.

CHAPTER SIX

STAYING MOTIVATED

Simon Sinek once said, "The hardest part is starting. Once you get that out of the way, you'll find the rest of your journey much easier." I agree, but I also believe staying motivated during the journey is a completely different battle that can unnecessarily *lengthen* the journey. In fact, I've seen it happen as a writing coach.

There once was one author I worked with who struggled with feeling confident about her work. She doubted anyone would have an interest in her story. She struggled believing that investing the time to complete her book was worth it. She couldn't see the value. And because she couldn't see the value, she lost her motivation. Once you lose motivation for anything, you may as well toss in the towel. Sooner than later, you'll back away from it and move on to the next thing. While I understand there's a time for people to step away, I also believe there's a time to push forward through our inner obstacles. We must learn how to motivate ourselves.

I can't tell you how many times I've heard aspiring authors say things like...

"I'm not a good writer, Kennisha."

"I don't have time to sit down and try to put my thoughts on paper."

"I don't know if anyone will read my book."

"I'm too tired at the end of the day and have no motivation."

These were her words and they are words I hear more often than I care to admit.

Common obstacles that damper our self-motivation

Being motivated comes easy for some but doesn't for others. I can't explain why this appears to be true. We can speculate that fear is the main culprit, but I believe that for many the unknown is a scary place. And if you're an author without a large platform you may wrestle with the concerns I mentioned. After all, as with most fears, it's easier to succumb to them than to fight them, right? Insert sarcastic grin. Obviously, I want you to shout "No!" face your fears head-on, and conquer them. But in order to conquer them, you have to acknowledge them and create a strategy. A part of that strategy is self-motivation.

Helping children get motivated to read

I am an adjunct professor at McLennan Community College. I was recently invited to be one of the Kids College instructors. The Kids College program was created to provide interactive courses for students who are available on Fridays. Since McLennan County has schools that only have four classroom days, McLennan Community College provides opportunities for interactive learning for students who have Fridays off and would be able to attend. I was invited because the course that I teach on book publishing could also benefit children who have an interest in reading and creative writing. Children enjoy reading, children enjoy drawing and illustrations, and I believed creating a lesson plan geared toward them would be the perfect opportunity to teach children how to publish books, how to create them and the elements of storytelling. I also hoped this would reignite their excitement about books again.

During one of the courses I thought it would be a good idea to talk about reading obstacles and challenges and to learn where the kids stood as it relates to their motivation to read. After reaching many elementary aged students in their classrooms over the past two years, I noticed that there are definitely kids that are interested in reading books, but the older kids appeared to have lost interest.

In my Kids College course, the first group of students were in grades 5th through 8th grade. When I asked questions like are you interested in reading maybe one or two people out of the classroom actually were interested. One kid very blatantly told me that he *hates* it because it's *boring*. When I hear kids tell me that they think reading is boring it's because their motivation to read no longer exists. A great question to ask is, "How did they lose their motivation?" If a child loses their interest in reading early on, just imagine that this child will become an adult who has absolutely no interest in reading...or *writing*.

In my class, we discussed their reading obstacles and I helped them discover strategies to overcome them. The same strategies apply to writers who struggle with finding motivation to write.

Write toward a reward

One of the sweet students in my class gave this recommendation when I asked the class how they can find motivation to read. She said, "Give yourself a reward." I love that children understand this concept. While it may seem to backfire- creating the expectation of a specific kind of reward every time- it can also produce great results and eventually introduce great habits, like finishing what you start and reaching goals. As long as it's clear that the reward may change (i.e. is not always monetary or the object of our affection), I believe this method can produce results when someone is struggling with motivation.

Rewarding yourself after reaching writing goals can have a significant positive impact on your motivation and productivity. Writing can be a long and arduous process, and it's easy to lose motivation along the way. However, by setting achievable goals and rewarding yourself when you reach them, you can stay motivated and on track. Rewards can be anything from a small treat like a piece of chocolate or a cup of tea to a bigger reward like a movie night or a day off work. Whatever the reward, it should be something that you enjoy and find motivating.

Rewarding yourself can also help to reduce stress and improve your mental health. Writing can be a stressful activity, and it's important to take breaks and look after your wellbeing. By setting goals and rewarding yourself when you reach them, you can reduce stress and promote a sense of accomplishment. This can help to improve your mood and overall mental health. Additionally, taking breaks and rewarding yourself can help to prevent burnout, which is a common problem for writers who push themselves too hard.

By taking time to rest and relax, you can avoid burnout and stay motivated in the long term.

When I was a new writer, my reward was watching one of my favorite television series. I'd say, "My goal is to complete chapter six. Once I am done, I'll reward myself with my favorite show." This is simple, but effective. Now, I could easily forget about writing, turn the television on and watch my show. By giving myself a goal, which is something I know is important to me, I can use the reward as motivation to complete it. This helped me tremendously when I struggled with motivating myself to keep moving forward.

Keep your purpose in mind

At the beginning of the Kids College course, I asked the kids to tell me some of the reasons why reading is important. In order for someone to be fully invested in reading or writing you must be able to identify why it's important in the first place. The kids immediately shouted reasons why so I could write them on the board.

- Reading helps you understand information.
- Reading helps you learn and grow.
- Reading helps your imagination.

I loved their answers. Using this as a parallel to motivate you to write, consider the purpose of your book and what it will mean to your readers. Do you understand the purpose of your book? Why do you want to write it? How will it help readers understand your message? How will it help readers learn and grow?

As an author, it is crucial to keep the purpose of your book in mind throughout the writing process. Your purpose is the reason you are writing the book, and it will guide every decision you make from the plot to the characters to the tone. By staying true to your purpose, you can ensure that your book is coherent and effective in delivering your message to your audience.

Furthermore, keeping the purpose in mind will help you stay motivated and focused throughout the writing process. Writing a book is a long and difficult task, and it's easy to get discouraged or lost in the details. However, if you remember why you're writing the book, you can stay connected to your passion and drive. Whether your purpose is to entertain, educate, inspire, or challenge, keeping it at the forefront of your mind will help you create a book that achieves your goals and resonates with your readers.

CHAPTER SEVEN

BE YOUR OWN BIGGEST SUPPORTER.

As a child, I experienced traumatic events that negatively impacted my self-image. This led to a lack of confidence and insecurity, which was difficult to navigate. I struggled with accepting my appearance, avoided eye contact, and rarely smiled. My fear was overwhelming, and my friends started to notice my habit of walking around with my head down. It wasn't until years later that I realized the root cause of my sadness.

It took two decades to overcome these obstacles and regain my confidence as a woman and writer. I am grateful for the therapist who helped me unpack my challenges and walk with me through the healing process.

One of my counselors was surprised that despite my insecurities, I was able to write books and build a small business. The truth is, my passion to help others gave me the motivation I needed to keep moving forward. I became my own cheerleader and found purpose in helping others discover hope through my writing. It wasn't easy, but I refused to let my past dictate my future.

I realized that my insecurities were just a small part of who I am and did not define me as a person. I learned to embrace my flaws and turn them into strengths. It was a journey of self-discovery, and I am grateful for the people who believed in me and supported me along the way.

Building a small business and writing books were not just about making money or gaining recognition. It was a way for me to express myself and share my experiences with the world. It was also a way for me to connect with like-minded individuals and build a community of people who shared similar struggles and aspirations.

Fighting feelings with faith

I needed to face my emotional monsters with a strong support system in place. That's where my faith and my desire to fulfill my divine calling came in. My faith served as an inspiration and gave me the strength to persevere when I was ready to give up. Thanks to my faith, I was able to ignore the distractions that were hindering my progress and keep pushing forward.

In addition to my faith, I also found motivation in Hebrews 10:24, a Bible verse that encourages us to encourage one another to do good works. This verse gave me the motivation I needed to keep going and act as my own cheerleader. I realized that my calling was more than just a passion for storytelling; it was about serving others and making a positive impact.

Moving forward to serve others

Whenever I recount my writing journey, I hark back to my childhood. At a young age, I had a penchant for spinning stories and crafting books as presents for my mom. Seeing her delight in my creations instilled an indescribable sense of joy in me. This experience stuck with me through the years and taught me the power of storytelling and its ability to positively impact others. I'm grateful that this lesson remained with me all these years.

Writing is a powerful tool that can be used to help others in a variety of ways. Whether it's through sharing personal experiences, providing advice, or simply offering words of encouragement, writing can have a profound impact on those who read it. One way to use writing to help others is by creating content that is informative and educational. By sharing your knowledge and expertise on a particular topic, you can help others learn and grow in their own lives.

Another way to use writing to help others is by sharing your personal experiences and insights. By sharing your own struggles and triumphs, you can help others who may be going through similar situations. This can be particularly helpful for those who are struggling with mental health issues, as reading about someone else's experiences can help them feel less alone and more understood.

Finally, writing can also be used to provide words of encouragement and support to those in need. Whether it's through a letter, a blog post, or even a social media post, taking the time to offer kind words and positive affirmations can make a big difference in someone's day. By using your writing skills to spread kindness and positivity, you can help make the world a better place, one word at a time.

Can you please repeat after me? Here's what I'd like you to say:

- I was given an important message to share!
- I am a talented and gifted author!
- My words have meaning and will bless someone's life tremendously!
- The heart of my message matters more than the numbers!
- I can write and share my message, because God himself gave me the mandate!
- I was uniquely created with a divine assignment to pen powerful prose!

Self-confidence is a crucial aspect of being a successful writer. Believing in oneself and one's abilities can make all the difference in the quality of writing produced. Having self-confidence also allows writers to take risks and explore new ideas, ultimately leading to growth and improvement. Remember, self-confidence is not something that comes naturally to all writers, but it can be developed through practice and perseverance. So, whether you are an aspiring writer or a seasoned professional, always remember to believe in yourself and your abilities. With self-confidence, anything is possible.

CHAPTER EIGHT

SHARPEN YOUR WRITING SKILLS TO COMPLETE YOUR BOOK

There is a common inquiry among aspiring authors: will specific credentials help or hinder their career choice? Is obtaining a degree essential? Or is it possible to have a successful writing career without one? The answer is that it depends. Here's why:

While there are many successful authors who have excellent creative writing talent and have not obtained a college degree, some believe that formal education could be advantageous to a writer. It can help you improve your writing skills. So, if you're struggling with grammar, it's a good idea to take English classes or consider other professional development courses that address your specific needs.

On the other hand, some of the best storytellers and non-fiction authors became bestsellers without a degree, thanks to their natural creative writing talent and incredible stories. They shared their personal experiences, tragedies, and victories without the need for formal education.

It's worth noting that many people choose to pursue a degree for personal accomplishments or professional reasons. However, if you're an aspiring writer, don't feel discouraged if you don't have a degree. Pursuing a career in writing is possible without one. Society often places pressure on people to obtain degrees, making it seem like it's a requirement for a successful professional life. While it does have its advantages, there are other paths to a successful writing career.

Having a degree doesn't necessarily guarantee success in the writing industry. It's important to remember that writing is a craft that requires dedication, hard work, and perseverance. Writing is an art form that anyone can practice and develop with time and effort.

Another advantage of not having a degree is the freedom to write without the constraints of formal education. It allows writers to take more risks, experiment with different writing styles, and create unique works that stand out from the rest.

Strategies to sharpen your skills as a writer

1. Attend writing or publishing conferences and workshops.

If you're an aspiring author, attending a writers conference can be invaluable. From resources, lectures, and workshops to fantastic networking opportunities, these events offer a wealth of benefits. You'll learn how to transform your book idea into a finished product, as well as how to effectively market and reach your audience. All in all, writers conferences can provide you with a competitive edge to succeed in the industry.

In addition to the practical skills you'll gain, attending a writers conference can also offer a boost in confidence. Meeting and connecting with other writers can provide a sense of community and support that is difficult to find elsewhere. Whether you're a seasoned writer or just starting out, being surrounded by like-minded individuals who share your passion can be a great source of inspiration and motivation.

Writers conferences often feature keynote speakers who are well-known and respected in the industry. These individuals can offer valuable insights and advice that you won't find anywhere else. Listening to their stories and experiences can help you avoid common pitfalls and mistakes, and provide you with a roadmap for success.

Attending a writers conference can be a lot of fun! It's a chance to get away from your desk and immerse yourself in a world of creativity and imagination. You'll meet new people, explore new ideas, and come away feeling inspired and energized.

If you're serious about pursuing a career in writing, attending a writers conference is a must. Not only will you gain valuable skills and insights, but you'll also make connections and have experiences that will stay with you for a lifetime.

2. **Join a writing group.**

When I first began writing, I researched and found a writing group located a little over an hour away from my city. They met once a month, and even though it was a bit of a trek, I made attending a priority. I brought my very first novel manuscript to the group, and their feedback and friendship taught me so much. I highly recommend finding a writing group yourself. Although meeting in person can create a sense of community, it's also worth considering virtual writing groups. This way, you can connect with fellow writers and gain valuable insights to hone your craft.

Writing can be a solitary pursuit, but it doesn't have to be. Joining a writing group can provide you with the support and encouragement you need to keep going. Not only can you receive feedback on your writing, but you can also find inspiration and motivation from others who are on the same journey as you. Plus, being part of a writing group can help you establish accountability and deadlines to keep you on track with your writing goals. Whether you join a physical or virtual writing group, you'll find that the benefits far outweigh the effort required to attend meetings or connect online. So take the plunge and find a writing group that works for you!

3. Read great books.

If you aspire to be a great writer, reading is an essential habit to cultivate. It's important to read the type of books you want to write. Don't hesitate to also read books on writing and self-editing. "Self-Editing for Fiction Writers" is an excellent resource to explore.

Reading is not only a great way to improve your writing skills, but it's also a great way to expand your imagination and knowledge. By reading different genres and styles, you can learn new techniques and gain insight into different perspectives. It's important to make time for reading regularly, even if it's just a few pages a day. By doing so, you can develop a better understanding of the craft and become a better writer. Additionally, books on writing and self-editing can provide valuable tips and tricks to help you improve your writing and refine your style. "Self-Editing for Fiction Writers" is just one example of the many great resources available to writers. So, if you want to be a great writer, make sure to prioritize reading and continue to learn and grow in your craft.

4. **Subscribe to literature specifically for writers.**

In addition to books and magazines, there are also countless online resources for writers. Websites like Grammarly and Hemingway Editor can help improve your writing by providing suggestions for grammar, punctuation, and sentence structure. Another valuable online resource is the website for the National Novel Writing Month (NaNoWriMo), which offers tips and support for writers attempting to write a novel in just 30 days.

Attending writing workshops and conferences can also be a great way to improve your writing skills and connect with other writers. Many conferences offer workshops on topics such as character development, plot structure, and publishing. These events also provide opportunities to network with other writers and potentially find a writing mentor.

Ultimately, the key to improving your writing is to keep writing and seeking out new resources and opportunities for growth. Whether it's through reading books, subscribing to magazines, or attending conferences, there is always something new to learn and ways to improve your craft.

5. Consider building a relationship with a writing mentor.

Writing mentors are people who walk through the book writing process with you. Although this is a highly recommended suggestion, it may also be challenging to find. Many book writers spend their time writing. They are creating characters, promoting their books, and walking through the publishing process.

That being said, there are still ways to find a writing mentor. One option is to attend writing workshops or conferences where authors often speak and offer advice. This is a great opportunity to network and potentially find a mentor who can guide you through the writing process.

Don't be afraid to reach out to authors you admire and ask if they would be willing to mentor you. While not all authors may have the time or bandwidth to take on a mentee, some may be open to the idea and willing to provide guidance on your writing journey. The key is to be respectful and understand that authors are busy people, so be flexible and open to their availability.

Finding a writing mentor may take some effort and persistence, but the benefits can be invaluable. A mentor can offer insights and advice that can help you grow as a writer and reach your goals.

CHAPTER NINE

THE IMPORTANCE OF GENUINE CONNECTIONS

When I first decided to pursue a career in writing, I realized that I needed a support system to keep me motivated and moving forward. Since no one in my immediate community shared my passion for literary publication, I knew I had to venture out and seek new friends. The internet seemed like a logical place to begin.

I stumbled upon Tricia Goyer's blog, "My Writing Mentor," while searching for ways to improve my writing skills. She quickly became a trusted friend and invaluable mentor. Through her blog, I met Mary DeMuth, whose blog "So You Wanna Be Published?" provided me with a wealth of knowledge about the publishing world.

When I learned that Mary was part of a writing critique group in Dallas, I eagerly attended one of their meetings. Sitting alongside other ambitious writers who were also pursuing writing as a career was an unforgettable experience that encouraged me to keep pushing forward.

Through the blogosphere, I connected with other writers and discovered authors and speakers who enriched my life. Some writers even took me under their wing and became personal coaches, guiding me on my journey to becoming a successful writer.

I'm grateful to still have a writing mentor who believes in me and sees my potential as I continue to pursue this career.

Here are a few reasons why connecting with other writers will help:

Writers usually understand writers

As a writer, I've discovered that those who are not in the industry have no clue about the amount of dedication, hard work, and sacrifice required to succeed. You may have heard the phrase "Anyone can write a book," but the truth is, while anyone can write one, it takes practice, skill, passion, and a willingness to learn to create a professional and well-written book that will sell. Writers understand the challenges of rejection letters, self-doubt, and the long wait that comes with writing and publishing a book. It can be a difficult lifestyle, but connecting with like-minded writers who "get it" can make all the difference.

Writing a book requires more than just putting your thoughts and ideas on paper. It takes time, effort, and perseverance to create a work that people will want to read. Even after finishing the book, the work is far from done. Editing, formatting, and publishing are all necessary steps that require additional effort and attention to detail. And even when the book is finally published, the work doesn't stop there. Marketing, advertising, and promoting the book are all part of the process. Despite the challenges, writing can be a fulfilling and rewarding career. The sense of accomplishment that comes with finishing a book and sharing it with the world is indescribable. And finding a community of writers who understand the struggles and triumphs of the writing process can make all the difference in the world.

Writing mentors help you learn who you are as a writer:

I once prayed for a writing mentor to help guide me and share their wisdom. Little did I know that several amazing individuals would come into my life to support and encourage me through some of my toughest writing seasons. For a while, I struggled with discovering my true writing identity and what sort of content I would produce. However, with time and great guidance, I have gained a clearer understanding of who I am as a writer and the type of articles and books I want to create.

Having a writing mentor can make a huge difference in one's writing journey. Not only can they offer valuable feedback and guidance, but they can also provide a sense of accountability and motivation. It is important to find someone who shares similar writing interests and values, and who can challenge you to grow and improve your craft.

However, it's important to remember that mentors can come in many forms. They can be fellow writers in a writing group, a teacher or professor, or even a friend or family member who supports your writing aspirations. The key is to surround yourself with individuals who believe in your talent and are willing to invest time and energy into helping you succeed.

As a writer, it's also important to stay open to new perspectives and to continue learning and growing. Whether it's attending writing workshops or conferences, reading books on writing, or seeking out feedback from beta readers, there are many ways to continue improving your craft. With hard work, dedication, and the support of a mentor or writing community, anything is possible.

Writers offer constructive criticism and wisdom:

I must admit, attending a writer's meeting and having my latest book project critiqued was a daunting experience. As someone read my work aloud, the other writers in the room began marking it up with a pen. However, I wasn't discouraged. In fact, I felt like a kid in a candy store. Why? Because I finally had direction. I could see my weaknesses and identify what required correction.

Professional writers are passionate about their craft, and the quality of literature and storytelling in their work is always a top priority. True writing peers will provide you with honest feedback and assist you in refining your writing. While receiving criticism can be challenging, it's one of the best things you can do to improve your writing skills.

It's important to remember that every writer has room for improvement, and even the most successful writers have received their fair share of criticism. The key is to approach critique with an open mind and a willingness to learn. Utilize the feedback you receive to grow as a writer and to take your work to the next level.

Building authentic relationships is crucial for any writer. By connecting with others in an honest and genuine way, we can gain valuable insights into different perspectives, learn from others' experiences, and expand our knowledge and creativity. Authentic relationships also provide a support system that can help us navigate the ups and downs of the writing process. Ultimately, making authentic relationships as a writer not only enhances our work, but also enriches our lives. So take the time to get to know your fellow writers and colleagues - you never know what magic may come from those connections.

CHAPTER TEN

OVERCOMING WRITER'S BLOCK

Writing can be a repetitive and mundane task, particularly for full-time writers who spend hours upon hours typing away at their computers. As a bestselling author once said in a news interview, "I don't like writing. I like to have written." For many writers, this sentiment rings true.

If you've found yourself in a "bad writing funk," you know what it's like to struggle to finish a chapter, blog post, or magazine column. Despite being capable of writing, you can't seem to find the right energy or passion to complete the task at hand. Writing becomes a chore, and the motivation to continue fades away. It's not writer's block, but rather a sense of stagnancy and fatigue that plagues writers.

Fortunately, there are ways to overcome this feeling of burnout and reignite your passion for writing. One way is to take a break from writing altogether. This may seem counterintuitive, but sometimes stepping away from your computer and engaging in other activities can help you come back to your writing with fresh eyes and renewed inspiration.

Another approach is to change your writing environment. If you've been writing in the same spot for weeks or months on end, it's possible that the monotony of your surroundings is affecting your creativity. Consider writing in a new location, such as a coffee shop or park, or even rearranging your workspace to create a new atmosphere.

Consider trying new writing techniques or experimenting with different genres. Sometimes, writing in a new style or on a different topic can help you break out of a writing rut and reignite your passion for the craft.

Remember, writing is a journey, and it's natural to experience periods of burnout and stagnancy. But by taking breaks, changing your environment, and trying new things, you can overcome these obstacles and continue to grow as a writer.

Re-examine the purpose and value of your writing project.

Writing a project can be a challenging undertaking, and it's natural to lose sight of its purpose and value along the way. However, it's important to take a step back and re-discover the meaning behind your writing project. To do this, start by reminding yourself of your initial motivation for starting the project. What inspired you to write about this topic? What message did you want to convey to your audience?

Once you've reconnected with your initial motivation, take some time to reflect on how your writing project can bring value to your readers. Think about what your readers might gain from reading your work. Will they learn something new? Will they be entertained? Will they be inspired to take action?

Another way to re-discover the purpose and value of your writing project is to seek feedback from others. Share your work with trusted friends or colleagues and ask for their honest opinions. Sometimes, an outsider's perspective can help you see your work in a new light and give you a renewed sense of purpose.

Make a Promise to See Things Through

Committing to finishing your book is an important step in achieving your goals as a writer. Not only does it demonstrate your dedication to your craft, but it also helps you develop discipline and the ability to see a project through to completion. Finishing your book can be a daunting task, but it can also be incredibly rewarding. You will have created something that is uniquely yours and that you can be proud of. Additionally, finishing your book can open up new opportunities for you as a writer, including the possibility of publishing or sharing your work with others. So, if you're on the fence about whether or not to commit to finishing your book, remember that the benefits are numerous and that the satisfaction of completing your project will be well worth the effort.

Of course, committing to finishing your book is easier said than done. Many writers struggle with writer's block, lack of motivation, or simply feeling overwhelmed by the scope of their project. To overcome these obstacles, it can be helpful to break your book down into smaller, more manageable tasks. Set achievable goals for yourself, such as writing a certain number of pages or hitting a specific word count each day or week. You might also find it helpful to establish a routine for your writing, whether that means setting aside a specific time each day to write or finding a particular location that helps you focus. Whatever strategies you use, remember that the key is to keep moving forward, even if progress feels slow at times. With perseverance and dedication, you can finish your book and achieve your goals as a writer.

Opening Up to Your Mentor or Coach: The Importance of Sharing Your Concerns

Writing is a challenging process, and it's easy to feel lost or overwhelmed at times. That's why it's essential to have a writer's coach to turn to when you need support. Sharing your challenges with your writer's coach can be tremendously helpful in improving your writing and helping you stay motivated.

When you share your challenges with your writer's coach, you're opening up a dialogue about your writing process. Your coach can help you identify areas where you're struggling and offer guidance on how to overcome those challenges. They can also provide you with feedback on your writing, helping you to refine your ideas and improve the clarity of your work.

Additionally, sharing your challenges with your writer's coach can be beneficial for your mental health. Writing can be a solitary and isolating activity, and it's easy to get stuck in your own head. Talking to someone who understands the challenges of writing can help you feel less alone and more connected to a community of writers.

Take It Easy and Avoid Rushing Your Work

Instead of forcing yourself to write quickly, take your time and focus on each sentence, word, and idea. This can help you to break down the task into smaller, more manageable pieces and reduce feelings of overwhelm. Additionally, try changing your environment or routine to stimulate your creativity. Go for a walk, listen to music, or try writing at a different time of day. Remember, writer's block is a common challenge and it's important to be patient with yourself and trust that your creativity will return.

Another helpful tip to overcome writer's block is to brainstorm ideas before starting to write. This can help you to generate new and fresh ideas and prevent the feeling of being stuck. You can also try free writing, where you simply write down anything that comes to mind without worrying about grammar or structure. This can help to get your creative juices flowing and loosen up any mental blocks.

It's also important to take breaks when you feel stuck. Stepping away from the task at hand can give your brain a chance to recharge and come back with a fresh perspective. You can use this time to do something you enjoy, like reading or spending time with loved ones.

Remember, writing is a process and it's okay to make mistakes. Don't be too hard on yourself and allow yourself to experiment and make revisions. With these tips and a little patience, you can overcome writer's block and continue to create amazing pieces of writing.

CHAPTER ELEVEN

ACHIEVING YOUR GOAL OF COMPLETING YOUR BOOK: PROPER TIME MANAGEMENT IS KEY

One Saturday, I had plans to catch up with some close friends. It had been a while since we had hung out and I was excited to spend quality time with them. Our get-togethers were always filled with laughter, good food, and great conversation. Sadly, I had to cancel our plans at the last minute due to a writing deadline.

I was disappointed, and I confided in my husband, "I was really looking forward to seeing my friends, but I can't afford to miss this deadline."

Although it was a difficult decision, I knew that I had to prioritize my client's project over my social life. At times, this is the sacrifice one must make when running a business or writing a book.

It can be challenging to balance work and social life, especially when you are passionate about both. However, learning to prioritize is a valuable skill that can help you achieve your goals. It's important to communicate with your loved ones and let them know that while you value their company, there are times when work demands more attention. In the end, it will all be worth it when you accomplish your goals and can enjoy quality time with your loved ones without the stress of unfinished work looming over you.

One way to prioritize is by ***setting clear boundaries*** between work and social life. This means deciding on specific times when you will focus solely on work and other times when you will be available for social engagements. It's also important to learn to say "no" when necessary, whether it's to a work assignment that you know will take up too much time or to a social invitation that conflicts with your schedule.

Setting clear boundaries is an essential skill for writers to develop in order to maintain their creativity and protect their time and energy. Here are some tips on how writers can set clear boundaries:

1. **Determine your priorities:** It's important to identify what's important to you as a writer. This could be your writing time, creative process, or personal life. Once you have a clear understanding of your priorities, you can set boundaries that align with them.

2. **Communicate your boundaries:** It's not enough to set boundaries in your own mind. You need to communicate them clearly to others. This includes family, friends, editors, and clients. Let them know when you're available to work, what your

turnaround time is, and what types of projects you're willing to take on.

3. **Create a writing schedule:** Setting aside specific times for writing can help you prioritize your writing goals and make time for your creative process. Whether it's early in the morning, during your lunch break, or in the evening, having a designated time to write can help you stay focused and motivated.

4. **Find your writing space:** Having a peaceful and inspiring writing space can make all the difference in your productivity and creativity. Whether it's a cozy nook in your home or a bustling coffee shop, find a space that works for you and make it your own.

5. **Don't be afraid to take breaks:** Writing can be mentally and emotionally exhausting, so it's important to take breaks when you need them. Whether it's a short walk outside or a longer vacation, stepping away from your writing can help you come back refreshed and ready to tackle your next project.

6. **Seek feedback:** Getting feedback from other writers or trusted readers can help you improve your craft and gain valuable insights into your work. Joining a writing group or sharing your work with a writing partner can also provide accountability and support as you pursue your writing goals.

Remember, writing is a journey, and it's important to be kind to yourself along the way. By prioritizing your goals, creating a schedule and space for writing, taking breaks, and seeking feedback, you'll be well on your way to achieving your writing dreams.

Another strategy is to **maximize your efficiency during work hours** so that you can free up more time for social activities. This may mean delegating tasks to others or learning to work more quickly and effectively.

For writers, maximizing efficiency during work hours is a crucial factor in achieving success. Here are some tips to help you make the most of your time as a writer.

Firstly, set specific goals for each day. This will help you stay focused and motivated. Write down what you want to achieve and prioritize your tasks accordingly. This will help you stay on track and ensure that you are making progress towards your larger goals.

Secondly, minimize distractions. This can be accomplished by turning off your phone, closing unnecessary tabs on your computer, and finding a quiet workspace. Distractions can disrupt your flow and hinder your productivity.

Thirdly, take regular breaks. It may seem counterintuitive, but taking breaks can actually help you work more efficiently. Taking a quick walk or doing some light stretching can help refresh your mind and prevent burnout.

Lastly, stay organized. Keep your workspace tidy and develop a system for organizing your files and notes. This will help you save time and prevent unnecessary stress.

By following these tips, writers can maximize their efficiency during work hours and achieve their goals more quickly and effectively.

Also, **don't forget to take care of yourself**. It's easy to get caught up in the hustle and bustle of work and social commitments, but it's important to prioritize self-care as well. This could mean taking a break to exercise, meditate, or simply relax and unwind.

Finding a balance between work and social life is an ongoing process. It takes practice and patience, but with the right mindset and strategies, it's achievable. And when you do find that balance, you'll be able to enjoy both your work and your social life to the fullest.

CHAPTER TWELVE

OVERCOMING WRITING DISTRACTIONS

In grade school, my mom always reminded me to stay focused. She repeated those words a hundred times a week, as I struggled to concentrate and fell prey to any distraction. Whether it was rain, hunger, or a blank sheet of paper begging for my doodles, I couldn't resist. Unfortunately, this habit continued into my adult life.

Even now, I have to work extra hard to stay on task. The idea of writing a full-length novel seemed daunting. Nevertheless, I was able to write not just one, but five books! Along the way, I've learned the importance of staying focused. To accomplish my work, I've found it necessary to turn off electronics, find a quiet space, and write without interruption.

Staying focused can be a real challenge, especially in today's world of constant distractions. With notifications popping up on our phones and countless websites vying for our attention, it can be tough to stay on task. However, learning to stay focused is an essential skill for success in any field. Whether you are a writer, a student, or a business professional, the ability to concentrate on your work is crucial.

There are many strategies you can use to improve your focus. Some people find it helpful to break their work into smaller, more manageable tasks. Others prefer to work in short bursts, taking frequent breaks to recharge their energy. Still, others find that mindfulness techniques, such as meditation or deep breathing, can help them stay centered and focused.

No matter what strategies you use to stay focused, the key is to be consistent. Make a habit of setting aside dedicated time each day to work on your projects. And remember, it's okay to take breaks and step away from your work when you need to. By finding a balance between focus and relaxation, you can achieve your goals and be successful in all aspects of your life.

In addition to these strategies, it's also important to eliminate any unnecessary distractions. This could mean turning off your phone or logging out of social media accounts while you work. It may also be helpful to set specific goals for each work session, so you have a clear idea of what you need to accomplish.

Another helpful tip is to create a work environment that is conducive to focus. This could mean finding a quiet space, using noise-canceling headphones, or even playing background music that helps you concentrate. Whatever works best for you, make sure your work environment is set up for success.

It's important to remember that staying focused is a skill that takes practice. It won't happen overnight, but with consistent effort, you can improve your ability to concentrate and achieve your goals. So, the next time you find yourself struggling to stay on task, remember these tips and keep pushing forward. Your hard work and dedication will pay off in the end.

So, what are some common distractions I should look out for?

1. **Television Shows / Movies**

I have a great appreciation for good movies, but when I need to get writing, I prioritize my workload. Typically, I'll compose a list of films to watch once I've met my deadline. Admittedly, I sometimes enjoy streaming movies in the background while I write, but only when I know it won't hinder my progress.

2. **Music**

Music, like movies, is something I thoroughly enjoy. However, when I'm in a dancing mood, I usually turn off the music. Instead, if I need to focus better, I like to listen to classical music.

3. **Social Media (Twitter, Facebook, etc.)**

Social Media is a horrible distraction for me. I have to silence all notifications. I also have to put my phone away sometimes.

4. **Issues / Concerns**

It's easy to get sidetracked by everyday household tasks and concerns. However, it's essential to focus on the work at hand. Give yourself permission to prioritize work over other matters to ensure you stay on track and achieve your goals.

5. Your "To-Do" List

Do you find yourself getting distracted by your never-ending "To-Do" list? It's time to find a new spot for it! Consider tucking it away in a drawer or folder so you can stay focused on the task at hand. Remember, taking on one project at a time is the key to success.

While there are numerous distractions that writers encounter, I have outlined five of the most prevalent ones. I'm sure that you can discern why I've included these in the list. In reality, there are many more distractions that writers must contend with.

CHAPTER THIRTEEN

CREATING A WRITING PLAN

A writing plan can help you break down your book into manageable chunks, making it easier to tackle one section at a time. By setting clear goals and deadlines, you can ensure that you are making progress towards your finished product. Additionally, a plan can help you identify potential roadblocks or obstacles, allowing you to address them before they become major issues.

There are several key elements to consider when creating a writing plan. First, determine the overall structure of your book. This might include deciding on the number and length of chapters, the order in which they will appear, and any sub-sections or headings you will include.

Next, consider the content you want to include in each chapter. This might involve brainstorming specific topics or themes, outlining key points or arguments, or organizing research materials or data.

Once you have established the structure and content of your book, it is important to set realistic goals and deadlines for yourself. These might include completing a certain number of pages or chapters per week, or finishing a first draft by a specific date.

Setting goals is an important aspect of achieving success. However, it is equally important to set realistic goals that are achievable within a reasonable time frame. It is easy to get carried away and set lofty goals that are beyond our reach, but this can often lead to disappointment and frustration.

Realistic goals are those that are challenging but achievable with the resources and time available. When we set realistic goals, we are more likely to stay motivated and focused on the task at hand. This is because we can see the progress we are making and feel a sense of accomplishment as we reach each milestone.

To set realistic goals, it is important to assess our strengths and weaknesses, as well as the resources available to us. We should also take into consideration any external factors that may impact our ability to achieve our goals. Setting realistic goals is a key component to achieving success. By setting goals that are achievable and challenging, we can stay motivated and focused on our path to success.

Another benefit of creating a writing plan is that it can help you stay motivated. Seeing your progress and checking off completed tasks can be incredibly satisfying and can help keep you motivated as you work towards your goal.

When you have a clear plan in place, it can be easier to stay focused and on track. You'll know exactly what you need to do next and how to get there. This can help to reduce feelings of overwhelm or uncertainty, which can be major barriers to motivation. Additionally, having a plan can help you break down larger writing projects into more manageable tasks, making it easier to make progress and stay motivated. So if you're struggling to find the motivation to write, consider taking some time to create a writing plan. It just may be the boost you need to get started and keep going.

Creating a writing plan is an essential part of the writing process. It can help you stay organized, set goals and deadlines, identify potential obstacles, and stay motivated. Whether you're writing a novel, a memoir, or any other type of book, taking the time to create a plan can help ensure your success.

Remember that your writing plan should be flexible and adaptable. As you begin to write, you may discover new ideas or directions for your book that require you to adjust your plan. By remaining open to these changes and willing to revise your plan as needed, you can ensure that your book stays on track and ultimately reaches its full potential.

CHAPTER FOURTEEN

REMAINING TEACHABLE IS KEY TO COMPLETING YOUR BOOK

I will never forget meeting Mary DeMuth for the first time. I was invited to a writer's critique group and was thrilled to finally meet her in person. Her beautiful personality and exceptional writing skills were evident from the start. As we sat in the cold classroom, I was intrigued by how involved she was, and I couldn't help but feel like I was in the presence of a celebrity.

The group watched a taping of an early morning news broadcast featuring Mary. I was impressed by her humility. When it was time for the group to critique each other's work, I was nervous, as it was my first time submitting anything for review. But as I discreetly observed Mary, I noticed how involved she was in the critique process. When it was her turn to have her work reviewed, she listened attentively to feedback and welcomed new ideas.

I was inspired by Mary's willingness to learn and her desire for growth. She taught me a valuable lesson that day -

the importance of being teachable. Even though she is an accomplished writer, Mary still values the input of others and seeks opportunities to learn and improve.

Critique groups provide an excellent opportunity for writers to learn from their peers. While the setting may be casual, everyone is eager to learn how their work can be improved. I submitted my work for review that day and received valuable feedback, which was exactly what I needed.

Mary often speaks about the importance of finding mentors and writing groups to help improve your writing skills. No matter how experienced you are, there is always more to learn. We should all strive to be teachable and trainable in this industry, as it is only for our benefit.

Regardless of your level of expertise, it is vital to remain open to learning and training opportunities within the field. There is always someone who can share valuable insights and help you grow as a writer. Embracing these opportunities will only benefit you in the long run.

As a writer, it's important to remain teachable throughout your entire career. Whether you're just starting out or you've been in the industry for years, there's always something new to learn. Remaining teachable means being open to feedback, criticism, and new ideas.

One of the biggest benefits of remaining teachable is that it allows you to continue growing and improving as a writer. When you're open to learning from others, you're able to expand your knowledge and skills, which can ultimately lead to better writing and more success in the industry.

Another benefit of remaining teachable is that it helps you stay humble. It's easy to become arrogant or complacent when you've achieved a certain level of success, but by remaining teachable, you're reminded that there's always room for improvement.

Being teachable means being willing to accept feedback, criticism, and advice from other writers, editors, and even readers. It also means being open to trying new techniques, experimenting with different genres, and stepping outside of your comfort zone. By doing so, you may discover hidden talents or strengths that you didn't know you had, and you can use those to enhance your writing and make it stand out in a crowded market. Additionally, being teachable means staying humble and recognizing that there is always room for improvement. No matter how successful you become, there is always more to learn and ways to grow. So, embrace the mindset of a student and remain teachable, and you'll be amazed at how far it can take you in your writing career.

Remaining teachable is important because it helps you build relationships with other writers and industry professionals. When you're open to learning from others, you're more likely to form connections and collaborations, which can be incredibly valuable in a competitive industry like writing.

Being open to learning and new ideas not only helps you improve your own writing skills, but it also allows you to connect with others who share your passion for writing. Whether it's attending workshops, participating in writing groups, or simply engaging in conversations with other writers, remaining teachable can lead to valuable connections and opportunities. Additionally, being willing to learn from industry professionals can provide insight into the publishing world and help you navigate the often complex process of getting your work out into the world. Ultimately, staying teachable is a valuable trait for any writer looking to grow and succeed in their craft.

Remaining teachable is essential for any writer who wants to continue growing, improving, and succeeding in the industry. So, no matter where you are in your career, make a commitment to staying open, humble, and willing to learn.

CHAPTER FIFTEEN

DISCOVERING YOUR AUDIENCE: TIPS AND TRICKS

"Your audience is one single reader. I have found that sometimes it helps to pick out one person-a real person you know, or an imagined person and write to that one." — John Steinbeck

Picture this: you're savoring a cup of coffee with a friend, and the conversation is nothing short of amazing. Your listener is fully engaged, inspired, and motivated by your words. You deliver precisely what they need to hear, and everyone leaves feeling satisfied by the encounter. Now, let's make this daydream a reality.

To bring your message to life, it's vital to know your audience. Established writers attest to this fact. John Locke, an author, believes that it's preferable to identify your audience before you even begin writing. "The best way to write a best-selling book," he says, "is to know who your audience is (and what they want) before you start writing. You should know everything there is to know about your readers in advance, and then write your book. Most people do it backward."

Knowing your audience is crucial because it determines the tone, style, and language you use in your writing. Your audience's age, education level, cultural background, and interests will impact how they receive your message. If you're writing for a professional audience, you'll want to use a more formal tone and industry-specific language. On the other hand, if you're writing for a general audience, you'll want to use a conversational tone and avoid jargon.

Identifying your audience will also help you tailor your message to their needs and preferences. For example, if you're writing a book about health and wellness for seniors, you'll want to focus on topics that are relevant to their age group and health concerns. Similarly, if you're writing a marketing email for a company's loyal customers, you'll want to highlight the benefits and rewards that they can receive as a result of their loyalty.

Knowing your audience is essential for effective communication. By understanding who you're writing for, you can create content that resonates with them and achieves your desired outcome. So, take the time to research and identify your audience before you start writing, and you'll be well on your way to delivering a message that connects with your readers.

Consider asking yourself these questions:

1. Who is that one person you're having coffee with?
2. What's his or her age?

3. Is there something specific about her that makes her your primary target?
4. What is it?

As a beginner in freelance writing, I wrote about anything and everything that interested me without considering my audience. However, after deciding to aim for publication in magazines, I had to learn how to pitch ideas effectively. To my surprise, publishers are interested in knowing the target audience of your writing. Without this understanding, you may find yourself directionless and struggling in the industry.

There's nothing wrong with exploring multiple genres or pitching article ideas to diverse publications. However, it's important to consider the audience you're trying to reach with your message. Ask yourself, "Why is this relevant to them?" Before branching out to other areas, it's best to focus on one and establish consistency. While some writers can effectively navigate various categories, it takes time and skill to develop such a reputation. I personally know award-winning authors who excel at writing both fiction and non-fiction.

CHAPTER SIXTEEN

ACHIEVING DISCIPLINE: TIPS FOR FINISHING WHAT YOU START

If you have aspirations to become an author, it's crucial that you have the discipline to see it through. As we've discussed in this book, writing a book is a challenging journey that requires dedication. One of the key qualities that authors possess is the ability to bounce back from setbacks and remain focused on completing their work. Resilience is crucial not only to writing your book but also to becoming a successful author in the long run.

As a book writer, it is crucial to possess resilience in order to succeed in this highly competitive industry. Being a resilient book writer means having the ability to face rejection and criticism with grace, and to persist in the face of obstacles.

The road to becoming a successful book writer is rarely easy, and rejection is an inevitable part of the journey. However, a resilient writer does not give up easily. They take criticism constructively and use it to improve their craft. They understand that every rejection is an opportunity to learn and grow, and they continue to persevere despite setbacks.

In addition to facing rejection, a resilient book writer must also possess the ability to bounce back from failure. Writing a book is a laborious process, and it is not uncommon for writers to experience creative blocks or setbacks along the way. However, a resilient writer refuses to be defeated by these challenges. They find ways to push through their obstacles and continue to move forward with their work.

Ultimately, being a resilient book writer not only leads to greater success in the industry but also allows for personal growth and development. Through the ups and downs of the writing process, a resilient writer learns to develop a strong sense of self, and gains valuable skills such as perseverance, adaptability, and self-discipline. In a world where success is often measured by one's ability to overcome obstacles, being a resilient book writer is an essential trait to possess.

Years ago, I was a ballet dancer and loved the art of ballet. Its grace, strength, and expression captivated me. However, I despised the practice that went with it. Even as an adult, my feelings were the same. I returned to ballet in my early twenties, and while I loved the feeling of stretching my arms and legs, I loathed the repetition. Every class, Madame Johnson would play her classical music and we'd start the same routine. I twisted and turned, extended and bent. The routine never changed. Despite my frustration, I soon learned that the more I practiced, the better I became. This routine became a regular exercise that improved my skills as a dancer.

Improving Your Writing Skills: The Golden Rule
Writing is an art form, and like any art, it requires practice.

The more you write, the more you hone your skills. Here are a few tips to help you become a more disciplined writer:

Journal: Keeping a journal is a great way to express your thoughts and feelings. Whether it's before bed, early in the morning, or during a mid-afternoon break, take some time to jot down your ideas. Not only is it a therapeutic tool for self-development, but it can also help sharpen your writing abilities.

Blog: Blogging is a wonderful way to build a platform and connect with like-minded writers and readers. It's also a great way to practice writing. Pick a topic you're passionate about and start writing. Or, write about random musings. The choice is yours. But whatever it is, write!

Create a New Document: Sometimes, the best thing to do is to simply open a new document and start writing. Is there a short story you've been meaning to write? Are you working on a book project? Want to pitch an article to a magazine? Start by jotting down your ideas. Then, make writing a habit.

Remember, if you want to improve your writing, you need to write more. Find small ways to write consistently, even when you don't have a pressing project. Don't overwhelm yourself; consider what works best for you and your schedule, and then move forward!

CHAPTER SEVENTEEN

SAVOR EACH CHAPTER, DON'T RUSH

One day, I walked into the gym, pumped up and ready to dive into a new workout routine. Despite having no recent gym experience, I was determined to start at a high level of intensity. I bypassed the treadmill and exercise bike, opting instead for a cardio kickboxing class. I thought, "I've done this before, it'll be a piece of cake!" However, my lack of physical preparation quickly caught up with me, and I was left in pain and exhausted after the class.

The next day, I had an appointment with a personal trainer, but my body was in no condition to handle it. This experience taught me a valuable lesson: to take my time when starting a workout regimen. Jumping straight into high-intensity workouts is not the best approach, especially if you're out of shape or have not exercised in a while. I believe it's also important for us to take our time with our books too.

Writing a book is a time-consuming process that requires a lot of dedication and patience. Similarly, one of the most important aspects of writing a book is taking your time to craft each chapter with care and attention to detail. Each chapter is a crucial piece of the puzzle that makes up your book, and it is important to ensure that each one is well-written and engaging. Every chapter in your book is a vital component of the overall work, so it's essential to ensure that each one is captivating and skillfully written.

Crafting Your Book: Every Chapter Matters

Taking your time with each chapter allows you to fully develop the characters, plot, and themes of your book. This will help your readers connect with the story and the characters on a deeper level, making for a more impactful reading experience. Rushing through chapters or glossing over important details can leave readers feeling disconnected and uninterested.

Additionally, taking your time with each chapter can help you avoid common pitfalls such as plot holes, inconsistent character development, and poorly executed themes. By taking the time to carefully plan and write each chapter, you can ensure that your book is well-structured and cohesive. By taking the time to fully flesh out each chapter, you give yourself the opportunity to explore different angles and ensure that your story flows smoothly from beginning to end. Taking your time with each chapter can also help you develop a deeper connection to your characters and their motivations, creating a more engaging and immersive reading experience for your audience. So, next time you sit down to write, remember the importance of taking your time and giving each chapter the attention it deserves. Your readers (and your future self) will thank you for it.

The Importance of Pacing Yourself to Reduce Stress

One way to reduce the stress of writing a book is to pace yourself. Pacing yourself means breaking down your writing into manageable chunks, setting realistic goals, and taking breaks when you need them.

When you pace yourself, you can avoid the stress of trying to write your entire book in one sitting. Instead, you can set small goals for yourself, such as writing for 30 minutes a day or writing 500 words a day. These smaller goals will help you make progress on your book without feeling overwhelmed.

Taking breaks is also an important part of pacing yourself. When you take breaks, you give your brain time to rest and recharge, which can help you be more productive when you return to writing. Taking breaks can also help prevent burnout, which is a common problem for writers who try to do too much too quickly.

CHAPTER EIGHTEEN

TIPS TO PREVENT OVERWHELM WHILE WRITING

Years ago, I found myself struggling to juggle multiple writing gigs, while also managing a household as a wife and mother of three. The constant grind of daily blog posts, book reviews, a book manuscript, and a magazine column was taking its toll. I had thought the writing life would be a breeze.

As I tried my best to keep up with everything, I realized something had to change. I was losing my *passion* for writing, and feeling overwhelmed with my responsibilities. That's when I discovered the importance of a structured schedule, choosing projects carefully, and making my priorities clear. By doing this, I was able to create some breathing room in my life - or margin - and regain my passion for writing.

Creating a structured schedule was a game-changer for me. Instead of trying to fit everything into my day, I set specific times for each task and focused solely on that task during that time. This allowed me to be more efficient with my time and made sure that I was giving each project the attention it deserved.

Choosing projects carefully was also important. I had to learn to say no to opportunities that didn't align with my passions or values, and to prioritize the projects that were most important to me. This helped me to focus on what mattered most and to avoid spreading myself too thin.

Making my priorities clear was essential. I had to be honest with myself about what was truly important to me, both in my writing career and in my personal life. By doing this, I was able to create boundaries and make sure that I was spending my time and energy on the things that really mattered.

Overall, these changes allowed me to create margin in my life - time and space for rest, creativity, and pursuing my passions. And as a result, I was able to regain my passion for writing and find joy in my work once again.

Tips for a Successful Writing Career Without Overwhelming Yourself

Creating space for your goals is key to achieving them. Here are some tips to help you manage your writing career without burning out:

Be Realistic: If you're writing a book or looking for freelance writing gigs, make sure to set a realistic time frame that fits your lifestyle. Don't overcrowd your day. It's important to find a balance between your writing goals and your personal life. Taking breaks throughout the day can help you avoid burnout and improve your overall productivity. You should also consider your energy levels throughout the day and plan your writing schedule accordingly. Remember, writing should be enjoyable and not feel like a chore, so it's important to find a schedule that works for you. By setting realistic goals and sticking to a manageable timeframe, you'll be able to write more efficiently and effectively.

Learn to Say No: Don't overextend yourself by saying yes to every project that comes your way. Carefully consider if you have the capacity to handle it, and if you don't, it's okay to say no.

It's important to prioritize your workload and manage your time effectively in order to maintain a healthy work-life balance. Saying no can be difficult, especially if you're worried about disappointing others or missing out on opportunities. However, it's important to remember that taking on too much can lead to burnout and negatively impact your productivity.

When evaluating whether or not to accept a project, consider the resources you have available, including time, energy, and expertise. It's also important to take into account any other commitments you may have, both personal and professional. Remember that it's better to do a few things well than to do many things poorly.

If you find yourself in a situation where you have already taken on too much, don't be afraid to ask for help or delegate tasks to others. Prioritizing self-care and setting reasonable boundaries can help you maintain a healthy and sustainable workload. Remember, it's okay to say no – your well-being and productivity depend on it.

Set a Schedule: Use the calendar on your smartphone or computer to create a schedule that works for you. This way, you can stay organized and on track.

There are many benefits to using a digital calendar. Firstly, it can sync across multiple devices, making it easy to access your schedule no matter where you are. You can also set reminders and alerts to make sure you don't forget important tasks or appointments.

Another advantage of using a digital calendar is that you can easily make changes and adjustments to your schedule. If something comes up that requires your attention, you can quickly move appointments or deadlines around to accommodate it.

Finally, using a digital calendar can help reduce stress and anxiety. By having a clear overview of your schedule, you can feel more in control of your time and be less likely to feel overwhelmed by your workload.

Overall, using a digital calendar can be a powerful tool for staying organized, productive, and focused. So why not give it a try and see how it can help you manage your time more effectively?

Rest: Writing is hard work, and it's important to take breaks. Rest and recoup, and be sure to take care of your health.

In the world of writing, it's easy to get caught up in the endless cycle of creating and editing. However, it's crucial to recognize the value of rest and relaxation. Not only does stepping away from your work allow you to recharge and come back with fresh eyes, but it also helps prevent burnout and promote overall well-being.

Taking breaks can look different for everyone. Some may enjoy going for a walk, practicing meditation, or engaging in a hobby outside of writing. Whatever it may be, make sure it's something that brings you joy and helps you disconnect from your work.

Additionally, taking care of your physical health is essential for any writer. This can include getting enough sleep, staying hydrated, and engaging in regular exercise. When your body feels good, your mind is more likely to follow suit.

Even though writing may feel like a never-ending task, it's crucial to prioritize rest and self-care. By doing so, you'll not only improve your writing but also your overall quality of life.

Remember, you can have a successful writing career without overwhelming yourself. Take a deep breath and create a healthy balance in your life.

CHAPTER NINETEEN

EMBRACING YOUR WRITING CALLING

After publishing my first book, I received a lot of positive feedback from readers. Some were extremely excited, while others expressed pride in my accomplishment. However, one comment nearly shattered my confidence: "Well, anybody can write a book." This is perhaps one of the worst things you could say to a newly published author.

When I heard those words, I immediately responded, "Not really. Sure, you could scribble a few pages, slap on a book cover, and voila - you have a book. But a true author seeks excellence in every aspect - a gripping plotline, relatable characters, and a story that will touch readers to their core. Can just anyone achieve that?"

The fact is, with the rise of e-books and self-publishing as a respected option, there has been an increase in the number of books being produced. This may make writing a book seem like an easier feat than it was 15 years ago, but it doesn't diminish the hard work and dedication required to create a truly great book.

It's true that nowadays with the assistance of AI (Artificial Intelligence) anyone can *make* a book. However, the real challenge is in creating a work of art that stands out from the rest. Writing a book requires a tremendous amount of effort, time, and creativity. It's not just about putting words on paper; it's about crafting a story that resonates with readers, evokes emotions, and leaves a lasting impact.

Being an author is not an easy path. It involves countless hours of writing, editing, and revising. It requires a willingness to take risks and put yourself out there, knowing that not everyone will appreciate your work. But it also offers the opportunity to connect with readers, to share your voice and your vision with the world.

So the next time you encounter a newly published author, don't belittle their achievement. Instead, congratulate them on their hard work and dedication. Recognize the effort that went into creating their book, and appreciate the unique perspective they bring to the literary world.

Navigating the Tough Path to Writing a Book: Insights from a Professional Coach

As a Book Writing Coach, I always strive to be realistic with my clients. The journey to publication is anything but a walk in the park. Writing a book takes a lot of grit and determination. It's a challenging undertaking that requires unwavering commitment, and it's not for the faint-hearted. Very few take the leap, but those who do know the effort it takes.

Whether you're an independently published author or working with a traditional publisher, you may face numerous setbacks that your close circle may not understand. You may have to deal with rejections that challenge your confidence and test your faith in your abilities. The uncertainties that come with book writing can make you feel insignificant and unworthy of the task at hand. However, just like the inevitable suffering we experience in life, book writing has its ups and downs.

My role as a coach is not to sugarcoat the challenges that come with book writing. Instead, I encourage aspiring writers to focus on the joy that writing can bring and to work hard to achieve their dreams in spite of the obstacles. Book writing is a gift and a calling, and some people are uniquely designed for it. I believe that real writers have a passion for writing that they can't ignore. It's one of our greatest attributes in our careers and what drives us to succeed.

Aspiring authors must ask themselves why they want to write a book. It's a question I often pose to my clients, and their answers help me determine if they have the passion and calling required to succeed in this challenging but rewarding field.

CHAPTER TWENTY

A GUIDE TO MAKING MONEY AS A WRITER

Despite popular belief, being a writer or author doesn't necessarily equate to being wealthy. While it's possible to earn a comfortable income through writing, it requires dedication and hard work. Many writers face the challenge of having to maintain a day job while pursuing their writing career. This means juggling two demanding roles and finding the time and energy to write in between. It can be a daunting task, but for those who are passionate about writing, it's a sacrifice worth making.

In addition to the time commitment, writers also face the challenge of finding a publisher or agent who is interested in their work. This can be a long and frustrating process, with many rejection letters along the way. However, with persistence and a willingness to learn and improve, writers can eventually find success.

Even with success, writing is not a career that guarantees financial stability. Royalties from book sales can fluctuate, and advances for new projects may not always be substantial. However, writing can be a fulfilling and rewarding career for those who are passionate about it. It allows for self-expression, the opportunity to share stories and ideas with others, and the chance to make a positive impact on readers' lives.

Ultimately, being a writer is not about making a lot of money, but about pursuing a passion and sharing it with others. With hard work, dedication, and a willingness to learn and improve, anyone can become a successful writer.

Here are some key considerations if you're looking to make money as a writer:

Writing is a craft that requires consistency and perseverance. Many writers have to juggle multiple jobs or projects to make ends meet. Moreover, the process of writing itself is often solitary and can be emotionally draining. It takes a lot of mental energy to create a compelling story or argument, and it's not uncommon for writers to experience writer's block or self-doubt.

Despite these challenges, writing can be incredibly rewarding. It allows individuals to express themselves creatively, explore new ideas, and connect with readers. Additionally, writing can be a powerful tool for advocacy and change. Many writers use their platforms to raise awareness about important issues and inspire others to take action.

If you're considering a career in writing, it's important to be realistic about the challenges you may face. However, with hard work and dedication, it's possible to achieve success and make a meaningful impact through your writing.

Determining Your Goals:

Decide whether your goal is to write for exposure or to earn money. If you're aiming to build a writing portfolio, writing for free may be a good starting point. However, if you need to pay for your basic necessities, then pursuing paid writing opportunities would be a better fit for you.

Ensure you have enough time to dedicate to writing. Treating writing as a full-time job is essential, as it requires a significant amount of time and effort. It's important to manage your time effectively and decide how much time you can commit to writing and job searching.

Job Searching and Networking:

Create a daily search-list of potential writing opportunities. Researching various magazines and online sources can help you identify potential writing opportunities.

Seek professional writing jobs with caution. Be wary of scams and research carefully before accepting any job offers. Freelance Writing is one online service that can help you find legitimate writing opportunities.

Consider starting your own writing business. This can be a lucrative option if you have experience in fields like editing or business writing.

Write short stories or informative works as e-books. E-books can be a great way to earn consistent money, but it's important to ensure that they are properly edited and have an appealing cover.

Setting Goals:

Establish both short-term and long-term goals for your writing career. Revisit and revise your goals regularly to track your progress and make adjustments as needed.

Remember that earning money as a writer takes time, patience, and perseverance. With dedication and hard work, it's possible to build a successful career as a writer and earn a significant income from it.

BONUS CHAPTER

WHAT APPS TO USE TO WRITE YOUR BOOK

We've come a long way since the Stone Age, wouldn't you agree? With technology advancing in leaps and bounds, it's no surprise that people are constantly glued to their phones whether they're at the airport, grocery store, or waiting for the train. As writers, we can take advantage of these advancements by utilizing the plethora of apps developed by experts that can greatly benefit us.

One such app is the Grammarly keyboard which helps writers to check their grammar on the go. It assists in identifying potential errors and offers suggestions to correct them. Another app that can be beneficial for writers is the Hemingway Editor app which provides suggestions on how to improve writing by highlighting complex sentences, passive voice, and adverbs. Additionally, Evernote is a great app to keep all of your notes organized and accessible from any device. With these apps and many more, writers can take advantage of technology to improve their writing skills and make their work more efficient. The possibilities are endless with technology constantly advancing and providing new ways to improve writing.

HERE ARE MY TOP TEN FAVORITE APPS FOR WRITERS:

Pages: Pages is my preferred app for creating files. It is easy to use and lets me stay connected with my Apple devices through the cloud.

Sticky Notes: Sticky Notes are excellent for posting random things that come up during the day that are not a part of my To-Do List. This helps me avoid forgetting important things."

Calendar: Calendar helps me stay organized and plan more effectively. Therefore, if you have an iCalendar, I highly recommend utilizing it."

Reminders: Reminders are excellent for managing small writing tasks that I must remember to add to my calendar, such as blog post ideas, links for further research, and article submission deadlines.

Blogging Apps: If you are a blogger, it's recommended that you have a mobile app for your chosen website hosting platform. Various options, such as WordPress, Blogspot, and Squarespace, are available, so it's best to search and select the one that suits your needs. Blogging can help you sharpen your writing skills and serve as a platform to work on your book.

Dictionary: The Dictionary app is perfect for providing clear definitions and more for your work. Download it today; it's a must-have for writers.

Goodreads: Writers can connect and discuss books on Goodreads. Join the community to improve your craft!

Dropbox: If you're anything like me, you probably have many files saved on your computer's hard drive. Downloading Dropbox will free up considerable space on your PC or MAC, enabling you to easily store larger files such as music, movies, and pictures.

Google Docs: Google offers a variety of apps that are ideal for writers. Google Docs, for instance, allows you to store your files, review them, and make edits.

Grammarly: Grammarly helps you understand your writing style and identify common mistakes. Grammarly is a great tool to improve your writing skills.

THANK YOU

Thank you for purchasing a copy of Put Your Pen to Paper. I hope that my book has inspired you to write and take the first step towards becoming an author. Remember, you already possess everything you need to succeed. Take your time, and write one word at a time.

If you're ready to take your writing to the next level, visit Create and Blossom Literary Studios at www.createandblossomstudios.com to schedule an appointment. Our team is passionate about helping authors unlock their potential, find their writing voices and achieve success in their careers.

Happy Writing!

CONNECT WITH KENNISHA GRIFFIN

Instagram: @kennishangriffin | @createandblossomstudios

Facebook: @kennishatheauthor

YouTube: @createandblossomstudios

www.createandblossomstudios.com